ISBN-13: **978-1-940927-33-6**

MAJOR STAR PUBLISHING

Imprint of Quincentennial Publishing Company

www.majorstar.us

A LIGHT OMNI MEDIA PRODUCTION

Published in the United States of America

Major Star
Publishing

Cover design concept: Lois Rooney

Cover design: John Errigo, PhD

30 NOV 2018

Dedication

Dedicated to my Mom, Helen Dreher. Thanks Mom for always being there for me!

"I have found that when you are deeply troubled, there are things you get from the silent devoted company of a dog that you can get from no other source."

(Doris Day)

Lost in Autumn's Rain

The wind sings and rustles the leaves outside my
window
The ones fallen
like puppies bounding
about my feet
Skittering across the lawn
Playfully teasing my imagination
With tales they are so ready to tell

I lose myself to the playful energy that surrounds me
And cherish the boundless excitement that
with each new tale
my Autumn casts her spell

Leading me in new directions
Filling me with love and awe
She is forever by me
I see things I have never saw

So come and listen to
these tales I tell you
To make you happy
bright and gay

As a small soul will fill you
and send you on your way

Table of Contents

Autumn

For Those Who Love Dogs

*I*t can rightfully be said that man has an affinity for our canine companions.

From the dawn of time man has craved companionship and our four-footed friends have provided friendship, protection not to mention a great source of amusement to we; their two footed counterparts.

Having a dog in one's home, no matter the breed, says something is very special about the person who chose to take on the task of caring for that stouthearted canine that now lays innocently at your feet. He who will be either a loyal guardian of home and hearth, or perhaps, a loving playmate for the children.

Whichever way, a dog changes the whole dynamic of one's true self. Lovely how a dog, makes you more selfless, and that being said is a very good thing.

The twinkle in their eyes and the absolute joy in their voice, is what I love about how people speak about their dogs.

People will lovingly share stories of their *fur-babies*.

They are obliged to show pictures of their beloved pets from the time they were chosen to hours before they left the house that very day.

Capturing the magic that makes caring for and loving the canine of their dreams that much more magical.

Within these pages are tales that will make you laugh, make you cry and make you wonder. As you too will understand just what it means to love a dog.

Enjoy,

Lois

New Love Born Out of Desperation

*T*here was nothing selfish or self-serving out of what I did. Just a wanted desire to continue loving the only way I knew how.

Unconditionally.

Sadly, our beloved Twinkle, our twelve-year-old corgi had passed away in my arms early Monday morning. The Family, Elizabeth, Mom and I were all heartbroken. We sadly carried out the task of sending her across that rainbow bridge.

Just two days later, Mom ended up in the hospital. She, sick with an infection and Lizzy and I were struggling to make it through the long day of waiting at the hospital.

We came home that Wednesday evening hungry and tired. I quietly made us both sandwiches and we ate in silence.

"It's quiet," Lizzy said. "Too quiet," I replied.

"I miss Twinkle," tears filled Lizzy's big brown eyes. "I know, I do too," and I reached over and hugged her. That little corgi filled us to the brim each day.

Even though her last six months were filled with vet visits and our heartache. She tried her best to always make us smile.

Now the house is quiet and sad.

Liz and I cleaned up the kitchen and got ready for bed. "Don't forget to brush your teeth," I'm going to call the hospital to see how Grammy is." I told Liz. Ok, Mom. Liz called from the bathroom.

After a quick phone call to the nurse's station, I went upstairs to my room, casting one more sad long look at the spot near the front door where Twinkle had passed away.

"I miss you baby girl," I whispered into the dark.

That night, sleep didn't come easily. I tossed and turned. In my mind I could hear the tune Twinkle - Twinkle little star over and over and over again.

I awoke in tears, pulled on a robe and came downstairs. Grief got a hard hold on me and I cried for what felt like hours.

Seated on the floor up against the front door I lost it. First the dog passing, now mom being sick. It was all so overwhelming.

Wiping my face in my sleeve, I tried to pull myself together. I know, I though. This place needs to be happy again. Really happy, playful, and noisy. Maybe, a puppy? It's too soon I tried to reason with myself.

But it's just too damn quiet here.

So, I grabbed my phone and looked up puppies for sale. I didn't want to choose another corgi. Seeing what we had just gone through with Twink and her loosing the ability to walk.

I knew I wasn't strong enough to do it again.

Something feistier that would love to play and be walked a real buddy of a dog.

I looked all morning.

Then I saw her.

A little puppy that looked too good to be true. A shiba inu. She was soft and perky and cute.

She looked like a stuffed toy.
I was hooked. Oh this would be a great present I thought for Lizzy's twenty-eighth birthday.

I couldn't wait to make the call about her.

Lizzy got up and at breakfast we talked about what she may have wanted for her birthday.

"I don't know," she said staring into her hot cocoa cup. "Do ya think you would like another dog one day?" I knew I was reaching but I wanted to try anything.

"Maybe," she said between bites of her pop tart. I began to show her puppy pictures. And stopped at the one I had seen.

"That soooo cute!" She smiled.

"It's a Shiba Inu; they come from Japan," I told her. "Look, she has a spot on her tail," Lizzy noticed. A round spot, an angel must have kissed that one.

"Japan," Lizzy repeated, "she could be like a dragon dog."

Lizzy loved everything dragon and at twenty-seven and her being autistic she had childlike qualities that allowed her imagination to run wild and in our world and **that was a good thing!**

"Kinda like a dragon hunting dog," I chided. Lizzy smiled. "Could we have one?" She beamed at me. "If it's ok with Grammy. I don't see why not."

I explained. "But we have to find out some things first ok?"

"Ok, I'm going to go take a shower." Lizzy excitedly finished her breakfast and disappeared upstairs. Moments later I could hear the water running.

I called the hospital. They connected me to the nurse's station on my mom's floor. I gave her name and waited. I felt a bit better over what Lizzy and I talked about and had hoped that today would be a much better day for my mom so I could talk to her about the puppy idea.

I was informed that my Mom was still asleep and she had had a rough night. Tears filled my eyes and I told the nurse I'd be up to see what was going on in a little while. The infection needed a stronger course of antibiotics.

We left for the hospital a short time later. I had decided not to bring up the dog issue just yet and to see how the rest of the day would play out.

We waited for a few hours and sat quietly in mom's room. Lizzy was quietly napping on a sofa in the room. I was gathering information about the puppy Lizzy and I discussed just a few hours before.

I couldn't just let this go.

"I want to go home," Lizzy stated. "I'm bored."
Lizzy got up and put her jacket on. She was through.

Waiting is the hardest for her but she was most of the time well behaved at the hospital. "Ok kiddo, I get it, let's go."

We drove back to the house discussing her birthday, Grammy, any many other topics. But, especially the topic of the new puppy.

Back at the house, I began to make phone calls.

First to the breeder, who was a soft-spoken man from Honey brook, Pa. We exchanged information. We spoke of the cost and how soon we could have the pup.

He informed me that she was one of four in her litter. She was seven weeks old she was due for her last Vet check-up, but we could come and see her if we wished. Well that was all I need to hear.

My spirit began to soar.

If mom was ok in the morning, I'll start telling her. At least that was the plan.

Lizzy and I played around all that afternoon with puppy names.

She had to be called something special.
I thought since her breed was Japanese she could have a Japanese sounding name. Liz liked the idea.

But what?

Lizzy and I talked about seasons, elements, and things we both enjoyed. Then I took to the computer to translate each word to Japanese. This killed a whole afternoon and at times made each of us giggle.

"How about Rain?" I asked her. "It sounded pretty."
"Nah," Lizzy said.

"I know," I said. "How about Autumn Rain?" I then typed it into Google translate and got "Akisame," it sounded great. "I like that," Lizzy smiled. "So I think that's what we'll call it if we get one."

"Akisame," she repeated again and again. She was hooked.

That evening we went back to the hospital. Happily we walked into my mom's room finding her sitting up and talking to the nursing assistant. "Oh, here's my Daughter Lois and this is my grand-daughter Lizzy." She seemed so much better. What a relief. We exchanged greetings and the nursing assistant excused herself so we could talk.

"What did you two do all day while I was sleeping?"
She looked in my direction.

"Just stuff around the house." I said.

"We looked at puppies on mom's computer," Lizzy's
honesty kicked in to overdrive.

"Can I get one for my birthday?" she looked at her
grandma.

"You playing all day on the computer and it too soon
since Twinkle passed isn't it?" Mom made the face at
me the one that said clearly she didn't approve.

"Well, I said. You're right it is soon but the house is
so sad and so quiet.

I just can't stand it. You've been so sick and we aren't
really going that far this year. I just thought a new
happy little soul would brighten us all up."

I smiled at her and gave her a warm hug.
We'll see, was her only reply.

I still didn't leave this alone. I made arrangements for
us to go see the pups over the upcoming weekend.
And put down a deposit I used my birthday money
from last year.

My best friend Kathy and her son Brandon were only too happy to spend a morning driving into the countryside and looking at puppies. The farm was only an hour from the house.

We had to be there before noon. While on the way the kids happily chatted in the back seat while Kathy and I talked about the puppy's name and getting my mom to agree.

"If it's for Liz's birthday how could she say no?" I exclaimed. "Lo, it's still a bit soon. I think I would wait a bit," Kathy said.

Maybe, I said quietly as I stared out the side window at the passing countryside. For a brief instant I saw Twinkle in my arms. My eyes grew warm with fresh tears.

Kathy's GPS got us right to the farms doorstep in no time flat.

The breeder father was waiting in the driveway and greeted us with a wave. The farm itself was immaculate. Every building painted white and wonderfully cleaned.

We stopped the car just behind the house. "You're here to see the puppies?" Asked a woman with a little girl in her arms as we got out of the car. "I'll get my husband one minute." She disappeared for just a moment.

"Hello, nice to see you, I'll show you the puppies." A neatly dressed young man shook all our hands and directed us to a building just across from where the kitchen in the main part of the house had been.

Inside the room was a raised kennel. The room was clean and orderly. We all waited for the man to return.

Then a door opened towards the front of the room and in came the man with two puppies in his arms another followed close behind.

"Oh my God!" Lizzy squealed. Beaming from ear to ear the pups ran all around the room. "I like the dark one "Brandon said. The one we chose with the white spot on her tail pulled playfully at Lizzy's pant leg.

"Oh Mom can we keep her?" Lizzy was hooked. "You can't take her today," the man told Lizzy she has to see the vet, "but you could come back next week and then take her home. She will be eight weeks old next week."

"If you leave a deposit you can pay the rest next week and she'll be all yours." He smiled kindly at Lizzy.

"Can we see the pup parents?" I asked. "Sure you can." He left the room with us playing with the puppies, returning moments later with a dark male dog and a tawny female each were about three years old and looked well kept.

The puppies ran and greeted them both.

"Oh Kathy, they're so cute," I said. "Go ahead Lo, you knew you were going to do it anyway."

I smiled and winked at her. Then pulling my wallet out I handed the man the deposit for the one we had chosen. "She's mine? "Lizzy beamed. "Yep!" "In a week we'll come back." I told Lizzy.

"I'll have all the paperwork ready next Saturday," the man said and we shook hands. Lizzy surprised him with a big hug and she excitedly got back in the car. We waved as we drove off.

"Now that's a great birthday gift," Brandon told Lizzy. "Your Mom is going to think you're nuts," Kathy teased. "How is she going to handle a new dog?" "We'll handle it. We always do." I said.

We drove back to the house after a lunch of fast food, which the kids seemed to enjoy.

We talked about the puppies and puppy names and getting all the things the dog would need and how to break it to my mom.

The sounds of laughter filled the car and for the first time in what felt like an eternity. It felt good to be happy.

Kathy dropped Liz and I off in front of the house. "I got to go" she said. "I'll call ya later and good luck with your ma."

"I'll talk to ya when I get home form the hospital." We didn't even go inside. We climbed into our car and headed for the hospital.

When we arrived we saw my mom sitting in a chair dozing.

"Oh, you're here I've been waiting. The nurse said I can go home today. Do you have my clothes in the car?." "Great," I said. "Ah no, but that's an easy thing to fix," I told her.

"We're getting a puppy Grammy!" Liz blurted out. "You are baby girl, really?" Mom looked in my direction. "That's what you've been doing all day? She asked. "Oh yeah," I said sheepishly.

I did not wish to fully explain myself here at the hospital, so I told mom. "We'll talk about it in a little while when we get home, how does that sound mom?" Mom smiled and agreed.

While they got all moms' paperwork together I went home and grabbed her an outfit to come home in. I quickly hurried back to the hospital. After helping mom get dressed, I listened to the nurse's instructions that were explained to me and soon we were on our way home.

After picking up mom's prescriptions and getting home we made ourselves comfortable. Pajamas and something warm to drink was in order.

"So, tell me about this puppy." Mom gently stared at me. "Grammy she's sooo cute. Just like a stuffed animal." Lizzy stated beaming. "Can I have her for my birthday?" "Please?" Lizzy hugged my mom hard.

Lizzy was the kind of kid that didn't ask for too many things unless she really wanted it. The fact is she didn't make it an issue but didn't let you forget either.

"You know honey we just lost Twink."
"Maybe we should wait awhile." My mom's reasoning was good but Lizzy wasn't buying it.

"Aww, come on Grammy, it'll be fun." Lizzy hugged her again.

"You sound like your mother!" She playfully told Lizzy.

I smiled in her direction as I filled each teacup with hot water.

She could never say no to Lizzy. Not if she knew it would make her happy.

"Well you two know I'm too old to take care of a dog. This will all be on you and your mother." Mom meant to get her point across.

"Can I have her Grammy?" Liz questioned.
"It's against my better judgment" mom said, "but." There was that pause. "Oh. Ok we'll give it a try."

She turned to me next. "Now you let me know everything about this new puppy."

The remainder of the evening mom and I sat in the kitchen as I filled her in on every detail about the dog.

She asked if I needed to pay for her up front.
"I needed to leave a deposit and we can pick her up next week."

I tried to read the expression on her face. This is going to be tough, I thought.

Mom wasn't always easy to convince and at seventy-six, she definitely was not as easy as she was twelve-years prior.

The next week flew by. All the chores for the week seemed effortless, as we got ready to bring home our newest hairy baby.

Lizzy's excitement seemed infectious as she drew pictures and asked repeatedly how to spell the new puppy's name. Mom too kept trying to grasp the pups name but it just wouldn't stick with her.

"Akisame?"

"Sounds like yucky, kind of" she smirked, "I wish it was easy for me to remember." Mom looked a bit confused. "I know, let's do this." I told mom what her name means.

"Autumn Rain, we'll just call her that."
"Simple right?"

That sounds simple she agreed.

Lizzy and I even made it simpler, we will just call her Autumn.

We bought the puppy a purple collar, leash and a nametag that could be engraved on both side. Akisame on one side, Autumn Rain engraved on the other. One pup, two names, but we will just call her Autumn.

By the time Saturday rolled around everything was ready. I received a call that morning from the breeder telling me the puppy was ready to be picked up.

I thanked him and said we would be there in a few hours the excitement was at a fever pitch for Lizzy and she couldn't wait.

We all got into the car and drove to out to the farm. The farm was in a pretty little farm community. Amish farmhouses dotted the hillsides. After an hour car ride we drove back up the same gravel driveway we did the week before. Mom dozing away in the front seat while Lizzy was happily listening to her iPod and holding the leash in her hands.

The young farmer greeted us as we drove up to the back of the house. "I'll go get the puppy" he said, as we all got out of the car. Moments later, we all gathered inside the room where we first saw the pups. I gave him the remaining money and he handed the puppy to Lizzy, which just nibbled Lizzy's nose. "I have her collar." Lizzy announced. It has her name on it. "And what is the name you picked?" asked the young farmer. "Autumn Rain!" Lizzy grinned. "Oh, that's pretty" the man said.

Good luck with her. Lizzy needed a bit of help with the collar. "Thank you," we all said. We climbed back into the car and waved goodbye.

Now our adventures were truly going to begin. But at least we were all together and happy. What a difference a few weeks and a few dollars make.

And we have a beautiful little puppy dog to make us all smile.

Midnight Run Away

*W*hat started out as a simple walk to the park under the lamplight, ended up being a mad dash around the neighborhood.

And here we go.

Autumn needed to go out. Ok, on goes the robe, flip flops and the leash and out into the dark. We slowly walk down the street bathed in the glow from the streetlights to the park at the end of the block.

Autumn doing what Autumn does while at the park. She nosed through the grass, chased an arrant leaf and peed. We turn to make our way back home.

Walking on the opposite side of the street. Autumn began pulling on her leash, seeing something moving in the grass.

All of a sudden I heard. **Snap**! The leash sprang back towards me and the little red dog was loose. Round and round she ran. Seeming to be elated by her dark side bolt.

Panicked I started to call her. "Autumn come," over and over, I shouted. Frustrated by it being dark. I banged on a door of the house at the end of the block.

Knowing that if someone just opened the door it would have helped. But no one did.

I tried my best not to get upset, losing her in the darkness. I watched her as she ran under a pine tree. Thinking I had her, I got down on hands and knees, Autumn on one side and me face to face with a very scared opossum.

The opossum just stared at me, frozen as we both watched Autumn as she dashed off through the backyards of the houses along the road.

I followed her, calling her over and over. Losing sight of her, I continued to call. "Autumn come." She raced along the sidewalk. She must have been thinking I was playing. Me, knowing her I tried to keep sight of her. I didn't want to chase her down to the Parkway.

Then behind me came the headlights as I turned around, I could see a spotlight shining. I stopped under a lamppost. Great I thought, the police. "Officer, my dog got loose," I told him as he pulled up along side of me.

"Was that you banging on doors?" he asked. "Yes sir, I needed help." Then another policeman pulled up. "Hey," he said, "**IS THAT HER**?"

Autumn pranced toward us in the light of the headlamps, playfully avoiding us. The officers started offering her pretzels and even their sodas to get her to come closer. Nothing was working.

The closer we got to her the faster she'd dash. Even another neighbor joined us to assist.

But over the course of an hour, the game was beginning to take its toll on the little red dog. She started lying in the grass panting heavily.

"What if you start walking home?" The officer suggested. I did as he said and began to make my way home. Autumn was still running though the yards but at least she was on our street.

Still she dashed along in the dark seeming to vanish from time to time. As we got closer to our house, the police officers were still behind me, and Autumn was far off to my right. I still worried this wouldn't work. "Autumn lets go home," I called. "Home Autumn."

She walked in the street beside me her tongue out visibly tired. I cut across the front yard and on to the porch and opened the door.

Then in she came, looking for her water dish. I quickly got her into her exercise pen.

I then went outside to thank the police officers for helping me."

Next time take your phone with you and call us instead of banging on doors," he smiled.

"I will and thank you officer," I said. I went back inside.

Inside, I walked over to Autumn's pen. I said. "You're going to be the death of me you crazy dog!"

I looked at her while shaking my head.

She lay there panting and looked as if this time she had learned something.

Or did she?

The End?

41

Where There is Silence There is Chaos

*B*eing awaken by a smack in the face in my opinion is harsh, but when it comes from your own child's hands it even more difficult to take. But it does happen from time to time. And this was how my Monday morning started. Ah autism, got to love it.

I redirected Lizzy into the shower and tried with all my might to hold it together. I quietly put Autumn on her leash, tied my robe closed around me and put on my sneakers as I walked out onto the porch.

The morning air was very humid for the beginning of October. "Let's go big girl," I said.

Autumn and I walked in the direction of the school at the end of the block. My intentions were to walk around the block and the get the day restarted as uneventfully as possible with little mention of the earlier incident.

While walking; I held a full fledge conversation with Autumn about how it really wasn't supposed to be this warm for this time of the year. She looked at me once or twice but was more interested in doing what she needed to do and playing with a leaf or two.

She was about twenty-eight pounds now almost full-grown size at eight and half months old. She walked nicely on her lead most of the time. I enjoyed walking her in the quiet of the morning sometimes it seemed like the only quiet time of the entire day.

We made our way back into the house and I set my sights on making coffee and laying out paperwork to do before the usual chaos began.

Autumn was in kitchen with me, she was quietly gnawing on a deer antler I had gotten her the week before. She seemed content as I poured myself my first cup of coffee and settled in to the work at hand.

Then came the all too familiar sounds from upstairs, "CAT'S OUT!!" Lizzy began shrieking from the upstairs bathroom. That could only mean one thing.

The lightening bolt that is our orange and white kitten, Chloe who was now free roaming about the entire house. She raced down the stairs and paused only for a split second in front of Autumn's pen. Autumn looked up and in a flash, she was on her feet barking to be set free.

"I'll get her!" Lizzy exclaimed. Liz flung open Autumn's pen gate and the chase was on around and around the two pets ran. Chloe was out maneuvering Autumn as she ran in circles around the furniture.

Lizzy roared with laughter, trying at best to grab at least one of the animals.

"What's going on?" My mom exclaimed as she slowly made her way down the hall.

"Cat's out Grammy, there she goes." The kitten darted back upstairs. Lizzy began following breathlessly behind both her pets.

"Oh this is a great way to start the morning," my mom commented as she settled into her easy chair. She turned on her heating pad and waited in silence watch and listening to the mayhem swirling all around her. I gave mom her morning tea and we both laughed.

Moments later Lizzy retuned downstairs, panting hard after chasing the cat and dog from room to room. "Can't get them they're too fast." Lizzy plopped down on the couch.

"Better luck next time." I chided. "It's time for chores." I said.

She made a face "Do I have to?" "Yep," I stated "that's the rules." "You want your allowance right?"

"Oh ok." She went upstairs to make her bed. I finally sat back down in the kitchen finishing the pile of paperwork I had laid out for myself.

I finished my work and had decided to go and take a shower. "I'll be down in a few minutes," I called to the others as I headed upstairs.

Ah... I thought to myself, a brief few quiet minutes to myself.

I grabbed my favorite jeans and tee shirt out of the closet and the few other things I needed and disappeared for a few moments of me time. Alone, having a few minutes to myself only a small break from all the morning craziness.

Emerging from my shower ten minutes later I was surrounded by madness in full tilt.

"Mom, Autumn has paper in her mouth," Lizzy bellowed. Paper, where is that from? I thought. The puppy raced passed me munching on what I could see as a brown bit of paper. I'll get her I shouted!"

Autumn thought this was a great game. She ran around and around the living room. I tossed a toy in her direction. She stopped and dropped the wade of paper and trotted off into kitchen with the toy in her mouth.

Grabbing the wade, I couldn't figure out just where the paper came from brown wet and sort of chalky on the other side. Hummm where did this come from? I thought.

Oh no, I know. I walked upstairs and drew back the curtains of the window at the top of the stairs.
Yep I was right. There was a four-inch gash in the wall next to the couch in the loft. And obviously claw marks. In the gash…the marks were **dog claws**.

"Lizzy put Autumn in her pen." I snapped frustrated. "And get that cat and put her in her room for now." I was ticked off at Autumn, she had gone a bit too far. Time out was her punishment for the day.
Now I had to figure out how to fix this.

I angrily drove to Home Depot to get spackle and a putty knife; I had some paint in the laundry room.
I recanted my story to the man in the paint department. "Ah puppies will do that sort of thing," he sighed.

"I know," I sighed. "We'll handle it."

I took the tools and headed home.
I walked passed Autumn in her pen scowling at her. "Silly dog," I snapped.

Then went upstairs with the tools to begin mending the wall. I worked in silence and didn't let anyone come up until I cooled off and the wall was fixed.

Autumn stayed in her pen the remainder of the day, only out for potty breaks and she was fed, playtime was out. I was just too angry to have anything else destroyed.

I had bought a spackle that was bright pink and turned white when it dried. I took the large floor fan upstairs with me to aid in drying between coats of spackle to insure a good mend. Then when the spackle was completely dry. I knew it was ok to paint. Not a direct match on the paint but it was the same color lot the paint store had told me. The spot was behind a curtain so I didn't care that much. It would do.

Autumn would bark from her pen from time to time trying to get me to soften but I wasn't having any of it today. "You stay put." I scolded. "You'll learn my girl, you'll learn."

The remainder of the day I finished my chores and after dinner, I couldn't take being the bad guy any more. Autumn looked up at me with her warm brown eyes and I could feel myself cave in. The evening news had just signed off. I walked over to Autumn's pen.

"Ah come on," I said, "enough punishment for one day, it's time for a walk." She wagged her curly tail and couldn't wait till I put on her leash.

We walked out into the warm evening air for our usual walk around the neighborhood. I proceeded to tell her that I was disappointed in her but hoped she would try harder tomorrow (at least try).

She stopped in her tracks looked at me and wagged her tail.

I think we're both beginning to understand each other. At least for the moment, I think

Tale of the Potty-Puss

*O*k, I realize now that Autumn is a rather assertive puppy. And that just maybe her hunting instincts are very strong in a dog like her. But today I think that ya might say just was an epic fail on her part.

The girls and I had just gotten home from running errands. The puppy was in her pen in the dining room, "I'll put Autumn on her chain for a few minutes" I said. Letting the dog out of her pen and opening the back patio door. I secured her on the chain in the back yard because if I didn't it was like trying to catch a small tornado for a length of time.

"Lizzy, I called as I came back inside leave Chloe out for a while." Chloe stayed upstairs in Lizzy's bathroom and bedroom safe from an over zealous Autumn most of the time.

But when the puppy was outside, Chloe had free reign to roam around the house. "Ok, Mom" Lizzy called from the landing. Moments later an excited explosion of orange and white fur bolted passed me. Chloe made a beeline for the shelf under the dining room table. Meowing in her own delight then racing into the living lighting on top of Grammy's easy chair.

From where I was standing in the kitchen I had noticed Chloe pulled her usual disappearing act. I guessed that Grammy's bedroom door was open and she was under or over something. Grammy was folding what was left of the laundry in the living room. "Where's the dog?" She asked glancing around the room.

"Outside," I answered. "I'll bring her in, in a second."

I walked outside Autumn was running back and forth watching a squirrel eating birdseed underneath the bird feeder in the neighbors back yard.

She danced around me as I tried to catch her on her lead. "Come on big girl, time to go in." She tugged as I pointed her in the direction of the patio door; I push the screen door open quickly and let her bolt inside.

"Lo the cat's out remember." Mom reminded. Autumn made a dash around the dining room table then headed in the direction of Grammy's bedroom. Then as quick as you could blink Autumn was heading up stairs, her footfall sounded like thunder on the floor above. You could tell she was racing from room to room looking for the cat.

Not finding her, Autumn bounded back down the stairs and ran around the kitchen and dining room table check for her buddy once more.

She dashed passed me again. And back into the back bedroom. I followed her. Autumn looked under each piece of furniture. She stopped short of the threshold of the bathroom and began to whine softly.
"Lo where's the cat?" Mom called from the hallway.

"Hey Ma, come here!" I started to laugh … "and grab my phone…would ya? I found the cat!"

Stopping just behind Autumn who was staring into the bathroom I began to roar with laughter.
There balancing inside the rim of the toilet, was one very cornered, very trapped orange and white kitten. "Meow," came her call from the inside of the toilet bowl.

"Where is she, where's Chloe?" My mom asked, "I am not really being able to see her very well in the dim light."

"She is under your potty seat," I explained, "hiding from the dog in the toilet bowl." We both howled with a fresh burst of giggles until tears rolled down our cheeks.

"Gimme, my phone, no one will ever believe this," I said, through my giggles. And I took her picture.

Soon Lizzy joined us and the moment she saw her kitten's unusual perch she began exclaiming; "Chloe is a potty puss!"

"The cat thinks it's a toilet brush!"
We all shared the best laugh that afternoon and retrieved the kitty from her soggy spot.

Drying her off and dodging the dog advances, "Guess you won't do that again," I said to Chloe as I cuddled her. She mewed in response.

Thank goodness the bathroom had been cleaned that very morning. And now Autumn has a new area to look for her little friend when all the doors are open.

Silly animals only go to show it's never a dull moment around here!

Years End

*H*appily I can say Autumn has turned out to be a pretty good dog for our house. She still has a few flaws to work on, like listening and her desire to destroy every throw rug in the house and turning the cat into a chew toy. But she is smoothing out. Her bond with the family is slowly forging. She is eleven months old now, almost full grown in size but has a bit to go to start losing her puppy ways.

I don't believe she could really figure out all the going's on about the Christmas holiday, wrapping paper, boxes the ornaments on the tree just high enough over her head for her to gaze at.

Or, maybe she was trying to figure why on earth we would put a tree in the living room in the first place. She did playfully pull a shatterproof gold colored ball off the tree and a good game of catch me going for more than an hour. So I believe that she may think this indoor tree thing is a great idea.

She also did get a kick out of me baking cookies for about a week.

Each time I got out the mixing bowls she'd come and sit by the island in the kitchen and wait to see if she'd get a small taste of an ingredient or two, or a cookie when it was all finished. Yeah, cookies are a very good thing in Autumn's eyes.

The one thing I know she enjoys is the music. Softly I'd play instrumental Christmas music while doing paperwork in the morning or while cooking or baking.

I'd put music on for her to listen to while the family went out on errands. She, safely in her pen in the dining room and dozing as the soft strains of holiday favorites or quiet classical played on.

Most of the time she was very well behaved while we were out at least so far.

I have noticed her pace from time to time. I wonder what she's thinking as I'm cleaning around her. Or is that her way of waiting for me to finish. Either way she is turning in to a real good companion.

Now and again, she seeks one of us out to play. Autumn's favorite game is fetch on the stairs when she can't be outside. I've taken this to a new level though. She's smart and looks at you like; "Is that all?" But I make her sit on command. Then when she sits I praise her, then show her the ball and ask her what is it?

She opens her mouth like she is trying to form words then yips like she is trying to say ball. I toss the ball softly to the next landing. Then she bounds up the stairs after it lays down and drops the ball. It bounces down each step and back into my hand.

We do this over and over until she loses interest. It's her game and we both enjoy playing.

It's snowed twice since Christmas and Autumn loves it. She stands at the patio door rings the bell hanging from the handle impatiently then bounds outside. She stares at the swirling snowflakes barks and makes a mad dash across the yard. Pouncing face first into the soft snow coming to the patio door again and again to be let in or for me to come out to join her. I do then she grabs her nearly frozen ball and disappears into the swirls of falling snowflakes.

I can only imagine what this new sensation is for her but she seems delighted. She, like a small child does what they all do. Runs in and out all day. She has to see the change in how much snow and how cold it's gotten.

Just like the game we played with our moms when we were children. Mom put my mittens on. Mom take my mittens off. Mom put my leggings on, Mom take my leggings off. Oh yeah, we played that all day when it snowed.

Mom would do this all day till we passed out in the living room watching TV after a multitude of in and outs and a hundred snowball fights. Autumn is no different.

She rings that bell on the door a hundred times. In and out she runs. Sometimes I wonder who conditioned whom for the bell?

The demands get just a bit more intense when the neighbor is watching her niece's dog Friday a black lab. Autumn can't wait to go and meet her by the fence. They give each other puppy kisses and each dash in opposite direction around the yards meeting back at the fence. Then they sit face to face like they are catching up on the latest gossip.

Friday was our old dog's best buddy. It took her a little while to warm up to Autumn and all that puppy energy but they seem to be friends now. Now, when Friday is around. She barks loudly and calls Autumn, the greetings and tail wags are always the same. I'm happy that Autumn has her very own friend.

The year drawing to a close has proved many new challenges for both Autumn and I but one thing is for sure. We have found love and companionship in each other.

Thought she is different from our old dog. She is proving to be a tried and true member of our family.

Are you Leaving Again?

*H*aving small animals in our house at times can be a challenge each one of us either human or animal has to adjust to the comings and goings of one another.

We have grown accustomed to all the day-to-day needs of each member of our household.

But when it comes to traveling, well that all together a different story.

Just after Thanksgiving, I had decided that the over indulgence of Christmas gifts was just ridiculous. We have enough of everything in our home that makes it comfortable and well supplied to meet each and every needed food, clothes, toys, movies, etc. What we really need was more experiences.

Going and doing. Us smiling all day.

Not just the day to day.

So, with that said and the conversation that ended with me calling the travel agent and set up a six-day trip. We were well on our way to our next set of experiences. Now, I had to groom the two critters into this new phase. Traveling 101.

Unfortunately traveling isn't a thing that Autumn does very well. The very few car rides she has experienced have resulted in more of a mess than a pleasure.

Oh yeah, carsick. She starts out fine, looking out the window her head between the front seats to see where we're going. Then all of a sudden. "Mom, Autumn threw up."

"That's gross ewwwww!!!"

Well that ended that day of running around with the dog. We ended up turning around and heading back to the house. Then, spending the afternoon cleaning up the back seat. Yuck!

But after two bouts doing the car clean out thing. I called Autumn's vet and they recommended that Autumn travel on an empty tummy. No problem I thought.

The holidays proved themselves as a happy mixture of joy and the usual chaos. The well laid out plans for the holiday meal. The calls to secure family friends were properly invited. The presents lovingly and happily made ready.

Then came the all-important call to the vet for the critters to be boarded.

I realize that putting a puppy and kitten less than one year of age in the vet's care for a week is expensive but it is with people I've trusted for years to oversee them.

They always took such great care of Twinkle and Sabrina over the years so these guys would be nothing new to them.

Quickly the holidays seemed to pass and the task at hand was to pack enough for our six-day trip to Disney World and a Disney cruise a well-intended gift I thought.

But, little did I realize I wasn't the only one with this train of thought in mind. My brother Bob had lovingly arranged an outing into the mountains for the New Year's holiday as our entire gift from him. His gift was also an indoor Waterpark to play and relax at.

Oh no, a double whammy for the hairy kids. Not just once but within two weeks of each other these guys were to be boarded.

I found myself having a full-blown conversation with Autumn about how it was to keep her and Chloe safe. Autumn sat next to me on the couch while I rattled on and on staring at me like she was trying to make some kind of sense out of what I was telling her. Her warm brown eyes seem to bore through me.

The twenty eighth of December came fast. We were all packed up and ready to go on what would be the first leg of our adventures with our hairy kids in tow, it was off to the vet's place. Autumn was on a short leash and Chloe in her carrier.

Liz carried the much-needed supply of treats and wet food for the weekend. And we were off.
This was our first leg of our whirlwind holiday shanaggins, heading up to the Poconos for the News years weekend.

Kalahari was an indoor water park and a real treat during the summer months. I couldn't wait to see how it looked dressed up for the holidays.

The hairy kids were welcomed warmly at vets' office, both were cuddled and instructions were given and contacts left in case of an emergency and we were off.

Spending time in the mountains of Pennsylvania around the holidays was a real treat.
My brother thought of everything. Our room was lovely and spacious; we had access to the Waterpark

all weekend and reservations were made for our New Year's Eve celebration couldn't have asked for a better gift for the holidays.

The only thing that was a bit off was the fact that it started to snow just as we had dropped the hairy kids off.

"We're still going aren't we Ma?" Lizzy looked out the window of the back seat and frowned. She knew I hated driving in the snow more than anything. "Yeah, kiddo we're still going, just very carefully. " "We'll be fine honey just stick to the turnpike and take your time we're in no hurry, Grammy chimed in from passenger seat."

"Mom I'm hungry, Lizzy added from the back seat. Ok I know just what we need. Quickly I pulled in to a near by fast food place still serving breakfast and grabbed a whole sack full of goodies to hold us over on our trek into the mountains. Everyone seemed satisfied and we headed on our way.

Nervously, I eyed the sky as the small snowflakes began to swirl around the car and dance in streaks on the road ahead. We'll be fine I thought. Slow and steady.

The trip took an hour longer than usual but careful driving got us to our resort destination in one piece. My mind eased as the girls meandered around the lobby as I checked in. Suddenly my phone ran the Vet on the screen, I answered it quickly.

"Hello?" I said. "Hello Mrs. Rooney, this is Katelyn just want to let you know Autumn and Chloe are doing fine and I'll be sending you video while your away. Have a wonderful holiday, see you next week." "Thank you Honey, see you then." I smiled into the phone.

Well that was nice nothing to worry about on that end. Now let the playing begin.

Happily I can say the girls and I played in the water, ate and celebrated all that weekend.

Me feeling relieved that our two littlest kids were being played with and cared for safely. It was a wonderful New Years

We said our goodbyes to waterpark adventure Monday afternoon and headed for home. Our plans to pick up the girls on our way ride home.

The weather had calmed down considerably and it seemed to be just as we needed it to be. It took us no time to get back to the vet's office to pickup the kids.

As Lizzy and I entered the vets we were greeted and asked to wait while the kid were brought out to us.

Moments later the excited wooing of Autumn could be heard as she tugged on her lead to come in our direction.

She looked 10 pounds lighter. "She looks great!" Yeah, Ashley stated she's blowing her puppy coat. So we took turns brushing her out. Autumn bounced around excitedly.

"Time to go home girl's," Chloe mewed impatiently from her carrier. "Grab your kitty Lizzy lets go home. Bye Mrs. Rooney, see ya in two weeks.

With a small bag of toys towels and leftover food and hairy kids in tow we climbed into the car. "Hi Baby girls," Grammy chimed as Autumn poked her head between the front seats. "Have a good stay?" Autumn began to pant and licked Grammy's cheek, A low meow can from the carrier next to Lizzy.

Back home at last. The New Year started the hairy kids readjusting into their routines. Grammy and Lizzy helping each day with the ongoing round of chores, while I prepared for the next leg of our adventures.

I made short work out of unpack, washing and reorganizing underclothes, bathing suits and warm weather clothes into a medium and small suitcase for the Disney trip ahead.

Autumn had begun to make it a habit of following me around. She sat and watched as I laid piles of clothes for each of us on the bed. Then as I turned to take the opened medium case off the floor I saw her. Seated prettily in the middle of the open black and white poke a dotted suitcase.

"Ha", I exclaimed think you're going along do ya?" I smiled at her she wiggled her tail her small brown eyes shining. Well they don't have doggies on the boat I only wish I could take ya but you don't like the water." Autumn cocked her head to one side and opened her mouth as if to answer me back but shut it again and stared at me.

"I know kiddo but it's only a week, then it's back to business as usual. "I went back to organizing the clothes for the trip.

I was excited but a bit more apprehensive about this trip. Ma wasn't always feeling her best and pushing her any farther than she was able to go was never a good thing.

I knew deep down inside that at least the cruise had staff at the ready if I ran into trouble at least medically.

Snapping the latches closed on the suitcase. "Ready or not here we go." I said out loud.

I just hope this doesn't bite me too hard I thought. We made quick work of putting the kids in the car. Chloe was in her carrier and Autumn on her short leash. Everybody climbed in the car and off again to the vets for boarding.

As Lizzy and I got out of the car and made our way back up the stairs to the veterinarian office, I suddenly felt the carrier the cat was in get very light.

Looking down suddenly the carrier was empty And a flash of orange and white dashed down the handicapped ramp; And was instantly hiding along the office wall behind the railing. I sprang in her direction landing on hands and knees between the ramp and the wall but catching Chloe by the scruff of the neck.

"Gotcha I cried, you little hair ball." Chloe meowed in protest. I cuddled her kissing her head as I got her back into her case. "Not escaping today my girl," I mused to her, "NOT today."

Lizzy and I stared at each other no time for the blame game. "That was a close one Mom, too close!" Lizzy exclaimed.

Inside the office it was business as usual. Feeding instructions emergency contacts and one last cuddle for each before our leaving.

Autumn pulled toward the door. She wasn't having it this time. You could almost feel her say I really just want to go home now! Ok?!

As I handed her leash to the vet tech. I had seen that look. It pulled at that dark place inside all of a sudden.

You'll come back right? You will ...won't you?

Six days later we did return, to fetch our furry children home and begin a whirlwind of new adventures.

We are nothing without these small souls that make our house our home.

An Ordinary Day

*T*he melodious alarm on my phone woke me precisely at five thirty in the morning. I reached blindly for the bedside table where it and my glasses were carefully placed the evening before. I just barely brushed the hurricane lamp and bathing the room suddenly was a soft pink glow. Autumn was sound asleep on her pillow just above my own. I watched her for a moment and wondered …just what does she dream about? I smiled to myself as I tapped the light again to turn it off. I grabbed my old robe and headed downstairs.

The air in the house smelled good, the scent of spiced pumpkin from the candles in the kitchen and air freshener I had put in the powder room, gave the allusion I had been baking. In truth, I had not, but I'll take it none the less.

I set up the coffee pot for my usual six-cup setting and laid out my paper work. Another busy day I thought to myself.

Just as I set down to begin writing out the day's ledger I heard a familiar bark from next door.

Friday, the black lab mix was being baby-sat. Moments later Autumn pranced into the kitchen and with a paw smack to the bell hanging from the patio door handle was demanding to be let out. With that came me being roused from my chair and letting the kid go play while I started working. "Hi Friday," I called. She sat on her side of the fence wagging her tail and barking in the direction of the patio door.

Autumn was quick to greet her by sticking her nose through the fence.

"You guys play; I've got to get something done before the whole house is awake." I slid the door shut and went back to my seat at the island but not before pouring that first blessed cup of coffee.

The weather outside had been hellaciously hot. I personally was sick of it. It was as bad as being too cold. All the inhabitants of the house were stuck indoors. It's just too unhealthy for anyone of us. I was longing for the cool of the fall days ahead.

I quickly finished my tasks I had given myself and decided it was time to decorate for the upcoming holidays.

The fall months have always been my favorite anyway so why not get started?

I cleared away my paperwork and headed up stairs. The attic steps were in my bedroom closet; I pulled down the ladder and headed up.

One by one I pulled down each box of decorations and the empty ones for the summer things. All are my treasures, lovingly kept and used from year to year.

Autumn watched with mild interest as I repeatedly took down dusted off and brought upstairs each summer item and wrapped it. I put seagulls, sailboats, lobster-cages and the like back in their respective boxes and then carefully pushed each box back up the attic steps to be stored until next summer.

I can only imagine what Autumn thinks about all the changes but she seemed amused with the entire stair climbing all morning long. I finished the complete autumn decorating in no time and it as off to the next task and it was just twelve noon.

"Ma, I'm hungry!" Lizzy's voice came from under a blanket where she had been camping out on the love seat all morning in front a wide array of Disney movies. "I know, how 'bout a pizza?" "Ummm, meatball is my favorite." "I'll get my flip flops, I'm starving." She moved a bit quicker when food was the main subject. I grinned.

I ordered the pizza before we even got to the car and was told it would be ready in ten minutes.

We climbed in the car and were off to the pizza place. A half hour later, we with a piping hot pizza in hand, we're heading back home to feed the hungry troops.

Coming inside Grammy had the table all set to eat and I was thankful one less thing to do.

"Now I'd like you to rest," my mom scolded.

"You've been working around here all day. Now I want you to stop for the rest of the day, alright?" She looked at me sternly. "Go take a nice cool shower after you eat." "Ok," I agreed. As I dropped the last of my pizza crust on floor in front of Autumn who picked up pranced into the living room jumped on the loveseat and preceded in hiding the crust in the throw blanket. "Silly dog we'll have ants as big as elephants if we leave that there." I picked up the crust and took it back into the kitchen breaking it into smaller bits and hand feeding it to Autumn one piece at a time. "Spoiled dog," Lizzy snorted. Taking another bite of pizza then she tossed a bite in Autumn's direction. "See, she likes it." Lizzy smiled in the dog's direction. "Yeah, but not too much," I warned.

The rest of the afternoon was a quiet one.

Ma decided that a long nap was in order. Lizzy had asked to watch a movie, while I proceeded to clean and clear up the kitchen.

Lizzy curled up on the loveseat while I then programmed a movie she desired. I returned to the kitchen. I saw Autumn wander slowly into the living room and she was deciding on which piece of furniture she felt like napping on and ended up jumping onto my recliner.

Walking in a circle and curling up like a fox, I knew she was settled for the rest of the afternoon.

I sighed and finished quickly. Then I myself, settled on the couch for an hour of mindless bliss.

I looked around the house satisfied with how everything looked. I was pleased that all were content and resting. I had to say all in all it had been a pretty good day.

The rest of the day proved to be pretty routine by standards.

Everyone showered before the evening newscasts. After the news, I took Autumn on her usual long walk around the neighborhood. Then back home for the usual one more TV shows, then meds for the girls, and then treats all around.

Then came our bedtime. Lizzy said her prayers in front of everyone. Grammy and I were repeating prayers along with her. Then it was upstairs to be tucked in. Autumn followed Lizzy and I upstairs as we called our goodnights to Grammy.

It was one more trip to the bathroom for Liz before the final tuck in and good night kisses. "Ma! Do ya really think Twinkle sent Autty here?" She searched my face. "Yeah honey, I really do." I smiled in the direction of Lizzy's bedroom door where Autumn was waiting.

We like to say Twinkle picked her, God blessed her, and Angels kissed her and sent her to us.

I kissed Lizzy again. "Now get some sleep." "Goodnight Ma." And I watched as she pulled the covers over her head.

I quietly closed the door and walked to the stairs. Autumn was sitting on the landing, "Ya know I said to her. It was a pretty good day." With that said, Autumn cocked her head. I raised my hand and she gave me a high five in response.

It was her way of agreeing. What a good dog.

Blessed be our ordinary day!

On Da Fence

*T*ypically when the alarm chimes at five thirty in the morning it takes me only moments to get up and get started for the day. But today I lagged a bit behind. Collecting my thought as l laid staring at the ceiling, Autumn snoozing peacefully beside me.

I scratched her behind her ear but she didn't stir so I sat up pulled on my favorite bathrobe and quietly made my way down stair. The floor in the loft was my only giveaway that I was awake as it creaked when I stepped on it. I quickly descended the stairs not wishing to wake the whole house.

These few moments were the only real time I had to myself all day so I could do as I wished for just a few precious minutes.

Coffee was first I thought, as I set up the pot and plugged it into the wall. It gurgled and the rich aroma filled the kitchen. I set up my paperwork and waited until there was enough coffee in the pot to fill my favorite cup than set off to start my day. I poured over the household ledger making sure that everything was paid and ready for the month ahead then set up for Lizzy's paperwork to be done for the day later. I being her paid companion, and this being My only real job it had to be placed in a spot that could be charted when the time we did our work was finished.

I was set for the day I thought.

Then came that oh so familiar bark from next door, Friday the black lab mix was being doggy-sat by my neighbor. I quickly heard Autumn race down the stairs and head towards the screen door to be let out. One tip of the bell and she bounded out the door and towards the fence to greet her friend, tails wagging as they touched noses.

"Well you two, I have work to do," and I closed the screen door and returned to my paperwork.

I could hear both dogs barking as if carrying on a well-worn conversation then I walked back to the door and watched as each dog taking turns racing around their own yard and returning to the stop they started and barked in triumph.

Friday saw me in the doorway and barked to get my attention. I just couldn't resist her, she was like a dear old friend that you just had to talk to so I walked over to the fence where she lunged up and placed her big front paws on the top of the fence and licked my cheek.

Autumn was at my side whining and pawing at the fence between Friday and me. Then with any warning Autumn bounced between the fence and me trying to get to Friday. As she came down her collar got caught on the top wire of the fence. The wire was held fast in the metal loop of her collar.

I grabbed her around her middle supporting her weight with one arm and desperately trying to unhook her collar with the other hand.

Autumn was in panic mode, so was I. I screamed for my neighbor to come help me but since it was so hot outside everyone had their air conditioning running making outside noises impossible to hear. One more thing that was equally frustrating as the fact my neighbor was a bit hard of hearing.

I clung to Autumn as she struggled and the tears ran down my cheeks. I forced her up just a bit higher and pushed the metal loop as hard as I could. It wouldn't come loose.

I needed a better grip I thought. I had to change my grip this meaning I had to let go all together. "Oh God help me," I wailed. I watched as Autumn panic filled eyes stared at me. "Hold on baby!" I cried to Autumn.

I then let her go she was hanging for a micro second as I caught her again and with my right hand forced the metal ring from under the wire loop of the fence. The dog's full body weight fell into my arms. She was free.

Relief filled me and Autumn licked my cheek no worse for ware.

I put her down on the patio where she politely poked her nose back through the fence and lick Friday's nose. "Crazy dog," I said as I looked down at her. Her curled tail wagging as she looked up at me. My heart was still racing but I smiled at her and rubbed her head.

"Lois, are you all right?" Kevin my neighbor on the opposite side of my house had heard me screaming but the whole affair was over by the time he had gotten to me. I recanted my story and he than apologized for not coming sooner. He was a mailman and was getting ready for work he said. I told him not to worry we were alright now. He said he was he glad Autumn hadn't been hurt and said he had to get going. I said my goodbyes and I made my way back inside.

Wow, what a morning I thought. If I hadn't been there I could have lost her, tears began to well in my eyes again. That thought chilled me to the bone. I walked over to the freezer open the door and retrieved two frozen chicken feet I affectionately called "chicky sickles" as a treat for each dog.

"Oh hell, why not for all that the two of them had been through this morning. I went back outside and handed each dog their treat. Autumn took hers to the middle of the yard plopped down and daintily began chewing on her snack."

And Friday had dropped right where she was and gobbled hers down in no time flat. I smiled at them both friends till the end I thought to myself.

I left the two dogs and returned back inside still shaken. This was a morning I'll never forget I thought as I poured myself another cup of coffee. And I bet it's one Autumn won't either.

About an hour later the whole house was wide awake and I recanted my morning adventures in great detail to the girls. Mom was alarmed but relieved that Autumn was alright.

My Lizzy's thoughts were that Autumn was a wonder dog.

For me I couldn't agree more.

www.ingramcontent.com/pod-product-compliance
Lightning Source LLC
LaVergne TN
LVHW051426080426
835508LV00022B/3253